LOST LEAVES OF LIFE AND LOVE

AISWARYA R MOHAN

Made with ♥ on the Notion Press Platform
www.notionpress.com

To the ones who were brave enough to be a lost leaf at least once in their life

Contents

Contents

Contents

Preface

I wrote my first poem when I was in second grade. I spotted a snake in my garden, and words just came to me, and magically I wove it into my first-ever poem. Unfortunately, that poem had a tragic end, as I lost the book in which I wrote it, and along with it, I lost a few other poems. I stopped writing poems and my focus shifted to quotes as I grew old. And later reached a point where I stopped writing. As time passed, my cousin and I entered into 21 days writing challenge and published our first book. And ever since the contest got over, I continued to write. I was careful enough to use google keep notes and have a secure backup. So here I am publishing my second book, and checking off my bucket list of being an author.

Most of the poems in this book were random midnight thoughts that came to me during my sleepless nights. There was a time when I would just erase these thoughts from my mind instead of writing them down. But now, times have changed. I make sure to pen down each thought. And if you are able to connect with any of these poems, or if you have ever felt like a lost leaf in your life, you should know that you are among the bravest souls on this planet and you are not alone.

Happy surfing through the pages!

Aiswarya R Mohan
aiswaryarmohan@yahoo.com

Acknowledgements

I would like to thank my parents for being my pillars of support. Thank you for encouraging me and for showering me with your unconditional love, throughout the ups and downs. I owe everything to both of you. Amma, no acknowledgement is complete without me thanking you for introducing me to "When daddy was a little boy" by Alexandar Raskin. Thank you once again for gifting me this book. I would also like to thank Kavu, for motivating me to participate in writing contests, without your motivation I wouldn't even be here.

I would like to extend my gratitude to my constants - Aparna, Navaneeth, Ameesha, and Syam. Thank you for literally being a call or text away. Thank you for always being there. I love you guys. I would also like to express my gratitude to my girlfriends – Tresa, Alphil, Ansu, and Enu, for always having my back, and for planning the best staycations and getaways when we all need a break.

I would also like to thank Malu, Divya, Selba, and Nanda, for giving the most honest feedback after reading my first poetry collection "Book of Unsaid Words". Thank you for telling me which poems were your favourite. It means a lot. Last but not the least, I would also like to thank NotionPress for helping me publish my second book and for making the publication hassle-free.

Dandelion

Have you ever felt sad
that the dandelion dies every time
it gets kissed by the wind
their love story is tragic
yet so pure
The wind helps the wanderlust
in the dandelion to travel to different places
before it falls to the ground
and dies

Band-Aid

The scars kept on coming

But he never got tired of being her band-aid

Sea

She was shy
She's a pale shade of blue
until she met the Sun
She roared mightily
and shone so brightly
because the Sea was kissed by the Sun

Kindness

Kindness is not just something the world needs
Kindness is something you need.
You need to be kind to yourself first
You deserve it.

Devil in Disguise

I thought he was an angel,
like a dream come true
But soon, I realized he was the devil
a nightmare in disguise

Terrible Truth

No matter how hard you try,
You can never escape from your memories

Shutdown

She didn't want her life to be a show
She closed the curtains
and shut the world, leaving it black
It was dark, and no one could no longer know
what was happening in her life
It was kept as a hidden secret

Mask

One day you'll no longer be able to
hide behind that mask of yours,
the mask will fall
you won't be able to conceal your identity
and the world would see
what kind of a monster you are

Let it Go

It kept on breaking her
She kept on holding on
only to realize that she should
break it before it destroys her

Pain

She swallowed her anxiety like pills,
Only to throw up her pain in the process

Hope

Hope is the one thing that stays,
no matter how many times
it gets shattered, all the broken pieces
gather together to become whole again
that's why we always hope for things to happen

Lost Leaf

Like the lost leaves
wandering through the sky
I was lost in my life
not knowing which way to go
and like the wind carrying the leaf
You supported me throughout my path

Terrible Truth

She was told to pen down
only happy thoughts
She smiled and nodded
the eraser knew her truth

Fallacy

All these years, I waited for a prophecy
so that I could figure things out
But I failed to notice that prophecy
was itself a fallacy

Him & Her

For him,
She is the Sirius
among the other stars in the sky
For her,
She is the butterfly
she fails to notice her beauty

OG Girl

She stood there, smiling wholeheartedly
while everyone was clicking pictures
She stayed there enjoying the view
because she belonged to the OG era,
for her, the best memories where
the ones captured by her eager eyes
and not by the ones captured by technology

Survival

While everyone was building their career
he was busy fixing himself
While everyone got a job,
got promoted, got a higher pay
he was finally able to
survive without antidepressants
He was the one you termed a lost cause
He was the one you termed as irresponsible
without even knowing what he went through
without even knowing his story
You judged him and talked about him behind his back
You failed to notice the suffering
You failed to be empathetic
he didn't care about your opinion
he fought his battle
and lives with the motto of
not wanting to prove his worth to anyone
because he knew that
he was worth way more than that

Bruised Butterfly

She tried to fly
But her broken wings
wouldn't let her
But she never gave up
She tried and tried and tried
And then one day
She rose into the sky
She was bruised
and that made her
even more beautiful
because she is a
Bruised Butterfly

Terrifying Thoughts

She was so traumatized
that she thinks it's impossible
to hope for happiness in her life
The world scared her

Dandelion & Wind

Falling for you was not
in my control
I fell for you the way
dandelion fell for the wind
like how in one swish
the wind stole the dandelion's heart
just like that I was floating in the air
on cloud nine, in love with you

Dark side

Everyone was enjoying the moon
bewitched by its beauty
While she stood there
numb, but at the same time
feeling immense pain
She stared at the moon
and she could feel the pain,
penetrating deeply into her heart,
traveling through her veins
making her tremble with fear
She was scared of the night
because of the wolves
who lurk in the darkness,
the dark evil homosapiens

Fear-Zoned

I took the less scary path
I took the comfortable path
only to regret in the end that
I could not come out of my comfort zone
I was Fear-Zoned

Mother

She knows how I feel
by just looking into my eye
She knows how I feel
by my way of responding
She knows my intentions
when I use my emotional blackmail card
She knows how I feel
when hunger makes me angry
She knows when I lie
and I'll be caught red handed
within seconds of lying
She knows how I feel
all the time
She is my most prized person
She is my mom

Hopelessly in Love

We defied gravity
as it was no longer able
to hold us to the ground
because we fell head over heels
hopelessly in love with each other

Devil's Love

Love is blind

Love is fierce

It's not a myth

Because she fell

in love with the devil

who is loyal to the core

Healing

Sometimes you need to cry
to fix and heal yourself again,
and others in the process
Like how the clouds cry
and the raindrops fix
the soil, grass, and plants

Father

Every time I feel sad
I know that I'll always have
one shoulder to lean on
I know that I'll always have
one lap to lie on
I know that I'll always have
my dad with me
throughout my life

Forgotten Family

We fed and helped them grow
only for them to leave us here alone
And they flew away to different places
leaving us parents here alone

Scars

Her cheeks were
as soft as a pillow
couldn't hide the scars
that wasn't as mellow

Snooze

The alarm kept on buzzing
and she kept on snoozing,
While one wanted a break
from all the buzzing
The other wanted a break
from the whole world

Eternity

As I looked into his eyes
I realized it wasn't a fairy tale anymore
it was our reality
A journey of two souls becoming one

Betrayal

When the sun kissed the sea
and died for the day
The sea waited patiently
for her lover, the Moon
Their love gleamed through the shining stars
and the Sun never knew about her betrayal

Beautiful Bond

She hugged him
and tears started flowing from her cheek
to his shirt and left stains
He hugged her a little tighter
He tried not to cry in front of her
because he is her super-strong super-hero
what bond is more beautiful than that of a
Father and Daughter

Lost

Like the lost stars in the sky,
I was lost in his eyes

Happy Pill

You are my happy pill
with butterflies, my stomach you fill
You are my happy pill
with happiness, my life you fill
and making sure nothing spills

Oyster & Pearl

You are the Oyster
and I'm the Pearl
You would break yourself
and you'd die before
You let anything happen to me
You are the Oyster to my Pearl!

Lost Love

It wasn't love at first sight
it was a connection,
a connection that formed gradually
without both of us knowing about it
From acquaintances to friends
to lovers, to couple
From being in a happy marriage
it all became deep gradually

But never did I ever imagine
this day would come so quickly
But never did I ever imagine
that my soul would be sucked out
But never did I ever imagine
that he would come back home
wrapped in the tri-colour flag

Lights

When the heaven lights kissed the Earth
I stood there
with my arms wide open
Hoping to view the Earth from above
just like the heaven lights

Nostalgia

There are days when I just stare at the moon
and lots of memories come to me
I don't know if this is a boon
There are days when I can't stop the tears
falling through my cheek
I don't know if this is a curse

There are days when I wished to drown myself
in the memories, I have of the people that I love
Because in reality, they aren't the same people anymore
but in my memories, they are still the same
they are unchanged

I drown in the emotions of the past
I drown in the nostalgia
and every second I think,
I ask myself the question
Do they miss me like I miss them
Did they ever love me like I loved them
Is this nostalgia true
or is it just happening in my head

Daisies

When the sunlight touched her soul
She bloomed as bright as the Sun
and no one could take their eyes off her
She bloomed as soon as she was sun-kissed
Every day she waits patiently for his kiss
One day he failed to show up and
no one saw her bloom again

Love?

For a long time, I thought
love was like a dove
calm and peaceful

But soon I realized that
love is wild
it's a hurricane of emotions

Warrior

There's no one without a scar
Some hide it
Some flaunt it
Some wear it on their sleeves

Each scar tells a different story,
A story of survival
A story of rage
A story of agony

Some are deep
while some are shallow
Some are dark
while some are red

In a world where people flaunt tattoos
Be a scar
Show it out to the world and
Be a warrior

And as days passed by
I too couldn't handle it
and I gifted myself with one too

A scar

Lighthouse

When it was dark,
and there was no light
I stood there
all lost and lonely
not knowing what to do,
not knowing where to go
Your bright beam of light came to me
You showed me the way
You guided me,
You lightened up my path
for me to walk
You are my lighthouse

Moon

She was the brightest one that night
and I couldn't take my gaze off her
She shined so brightly
and made everything else into a shadow
She gave a darker shade to the silhouettes
She brightened up the narrow dark paths

I looked around and realized that
all the eyes around me were staring at her
She's got everyone's attention
no one could pull themselves from gazing at her

Even with all this endless attention
She wasn't blushing
I wonder how,
there wasn't a hint of pink on her cheeks
I wonder how,
She was so bright that I envied to be her
I envied to be the Moon

Masked Man

He's a man of different masks
and to make people understand is a task

No one's seen it other than me
which makes it hard for them to believe
There are times when I wished to tear the mask
and ask him why he's hiding behind it

Maybe his pain changed him
Maybe he's suffered a lot
Or maybe this is how he is
Or maybe he is indeed a man of different masks

But who am I
to paint him as evil
But who am I
to paint him as a saint
But for me
He'll always be the man of different masks

Lost & Found

Like the lighthouse that guides the sailors,
Like the compass that guides the trekkers,
Like Polaris that guides the travelers,
You guide me through my life
Without you, I would be so lost!

Wish

Oh! I wish for many things,

I wish the old reminiscences

won't flood my thoughts

I wish to bewitch my mind

with only happy thoughts

and brush away all

the uncertain future thoughts

Oh! I wish for many things,

I wish for the chocolates from the Swiss

which is something I can never resist

I wish to kiss the snowflakes

and enrich my soul with love

I wish to wander off far away

and that would be such a bliss

Oh! I wish for the strength

to handle all the mighty waves

to handle the human rat race

I can handle the stitches

but not the bossy bitches

Oh! I wish for the strength

to not fall into the abyss

Oh! I wish for many things

Cloud

My heart is filled with futile thoughts of the future
Every second I feel my head can't handle the torture
I yearn for your presence
And you, my love
You make me feel better
You take away all my burden
You cast yourself like a mist around me
so that no other thoughts surround me

And you, my love
You make me feel as light as a cloud
You make me feel free

Because you, my love
You make my heart at peace
And make me live with ease

Dark Night

When all places are out of light
and everyone's out of sight
All I wish for is something bright
to light up the night

Unbreakable Bond

When the Sun feels gloomy
the clouds come to his rescue
they hide the Sun
while the whole world thinks it's
the cries of the clouds

Only the Sun and the Clouds
know the bond they share
it's unbreakable
While the whole universe thinks
the clouds are bawling
but the Sun knows that the
Clouds are his protector

Clouds give time for the Sun
to calm down and relax
to settle down and chill
by floating around and hiding from the Sun

And no bond is as strong
and unbreakable
as the one between the Sun and the Clouds

Things that I love

I love the little things in life
I love the little act of kindness

I love it when my mom tells me to be careful
every time I use the stove
I love it when my dad tells me to be careful
every time I drive the car

I love it when a stranger smiles at me
and it lights up my mood on a gloomy day
I love it when a stranger stops the car
and allows pedestrians to cross

I love it when I get to eat ice cream
on a warm sunny evening
And to eat a little more than a chocolate bar
without having to feel guilty about gaining some extra pounds

I love it when someone shares the last slice of pizza with me
I love it when I get my favourite food every time I fall sick
I love it when someone sends me a random message saying that
they miss me
I love it when someone stops their video game just to check on me

I love the little things in life
It's what makes life so precious

Shadow

We all have goodness and evil in us
the evil part of us, is in our shadow
As we walk into the dark
with no room for light
the shadow becomes us
and we become evil

Leaves

As autumn comes,

the leaves fall,

some would be all across the road,

some fly with the wind,

and some get lost in the course.

But as Spring comes,

new leaves take over,

but someone might be more fascinated

when they find a lost leaf from the autumn

that was on their doorstep.

Some might treasure an old maple tree leaf

in their fragile books,

and years later when they look at it,

it would bring a smile to their face.

Similarly, in love and life,

we would have instances where we felt lost,

but years later when we look back to those memories,

it would bring up a smile to our faces

because they taught us lessons for our future as well.

Freedom

All she ever wanted to be was free,
But she couldn't free herself from her thoughts

Home

While everyone was busy
finding a fancy apartment,
she searched for someone
who could make her feel home